Eleanor, Eleanor,

not your real name

Eleanor, Eleanor,
not your real name

Kathryn Cowles

The Dorothy Brunsman Poetry Prize, 2008

Bear Star Press

Bear Star Press
185 Hollow Oak Drive
Cohasset, CA 95973
530.891.0360
www.bearstarpress.com

Cover art by Kathryn Cowles
Interior collages by Natalie Green (1, 2, 4, & 5) and Brenda Sieczkowski (3)
Book design by Beth Spencer
Author photo by Geoffrey Babbitt

The publisher gratefully acknowledges Dorothy Brunsman
for her generous donation of the prize.

ISBN: 9780979374517
Library of Congress Control Number: 2008924901

Acknowledgments

"Interview" first appeared in *Pleiades*; "Eleanor" and "Eleanor is generous" first appeared in *The Hawai'i Review*. "Poem with a historical event at its end" was chosen to represent the University of Utah in the AWP Intro Awards competition for 2006. "No name #1" was chosen for 2008. A group of poems from this manuscript was chosen as a finalist for the 2007 Writers at Work competition. Many thanks to the editors of these journals and the judges and organizations behind these competitions.

I am eager to thank the Khazeni family and the Reza Ali Khazeni Memorial Foundation for their generous support, without which I could not have completed this book.

Donald Revell, Karen Brennan, Kate Coles, I am always thanking you, and I can never thank you enough. Thanks to my fellow writers and dear, dear friends Geoffrey Babbitt (of all people especially you, Geoff), Eryn Green, Nathan Hauke, Derek Henderson, Rebecca Lindenberg, Christine Marshall, Cami Nelson, Wendy Scofield, Ely Shipley, and Brenda Sieczkowski, for their help and encouragement with these poems. Thanks and love to my wonderful family—Dad and Mary Ellen, Mom and Phil, Kate and Alex, Cristie and Steven, Travis and Heidi, Rob and Erin, Steve, Jack, Marissa, and all the nephews—and my grandparents Cowles and Waite. Thanks also to the Watts family.

For their enduring friendship before, during, and after the writing of this book, thanks to Brooke Johnson, Natalie Green, and Rachel Marston. And one more thanks for Geoff, for love, for good measure.

This book is dedicated to Paul Cowles.

Table of Contents

Eleanor

4

5

Eleanor

the sun rose and there was Eleanor
as if always

1

my bare back on the wall via overhead projector circa 1979 transferred
to tracing paper

stars
for emphasis

swarmdarkblack

A vision

I sat down to write *Eleanor*
but the holy ghost
said to make a bowl of instant
pistachio pudding instead.
One must listen to the holy ghost
and the pudding was ready to be eaten
on account of its having nearly expired.

Song:
O green, green, living
green with pistachio bits!
O white powder that turns
green with unnatural vivacity
upon contact with milk!
O green, green, eat green, oh Eleanor,
so green!

About Eleanor

1) was small and is still for all I know
2) the wart under her lip looked like a beauty mark
3) was a beauty and is still for all I know
4) a beauty with a limp
5) was always dusted with dirt; during a stint at a bakery it was flour
6) could climb trees well; her smallness was an asset
7) one leg nearly always broken
8) broken or with a limp
9) brown hair
10) at least one of her bones came from a donor
11) legs unshaven, like trees in the wild
12) could ride her bicycle downhill when her leg was broken, but not back up
13) not a swimmer, but able to swim; superior floater
14) on Sundays we would float down a mossweedy stream and when churchgoers walked by, we'd duck under the water and breathe through reeds
15) they could still see us, of course; that was not the point
16) was a knitter; scarves and hats
17) one summer we planted a purple petunia behind some bushes in memory of our favorite swingset, removed for safety; we watered the petunia at night in secret until someone found it and pulled it up as a weed
18) green eyes, greeeennnn, with extra eeeees and nnnns; slivers-of-triangle iris her strongest muscle of all
19) needless to say
20) was allergic to cashews; craved cashews
21) was a painter and is still for all I know
22) purchased thrift-store paintings just to paint over the canvases
23) sometimes all white or all red or all green
24) was not really called Eleanor
25) that part's mine

Eleanor is generous

1
She gives me a Catholic upbringing.
She gives me a father who couldn't read
    and a grandmother with hard candies stuffed in her bosom.
She gives me a toy truck.

Eleanor gives me a butterfly net and puts on a butterfly costume.
She gives me a banjo and a clarinet and a song for two banjos and two clarinets.
She gives me a small number of grey hairs.
She gives me tap shoes and a part in a family song and dance ensemble.
She gives me a beating heart, a pulse to keep my hands warm.

Eleanor gives me a picture frame and a nod and a wink
    and another kink in my neck.
Eleanor gives my words the worst possible connotations.
Eleanor takes some back.
Eleanor gives me an apple and another apple.
She gives me more apples than I need.

Eleanor gives me a punch in the stomach.
Eleanor pays attention.
With Eleanor, one glosses over the details.
Eleanor gives one details to gloss over.
Eleanor gives me an umbrella in the rain; she is herself
    umbrella and rain and sun and bulb and hyacinth bloom.
Eleanor gives me the evaporation condensation precipitation cycle and a crayon
    picture of a rain cloud hitting the mountains and spilling its contents, which roll
    together and out to sea and are lifted up in little dotted lines into another rain
    cloud.
The cloud is heading for the hills.

2

Eleanor unfolds only to reveal more folds. She is not a sheet but thin. She is not an onion but circular and multilayered and sweet with an aftertaste that's sweet and bitter. She is not a hat but stays on my head. She is not a blanket but wraps around me. She opens and opens and retains her shape after multiple washings. She is not a box unless she is a box missing a lid, or a box that never had a lid.

3

It's nice to sit.
Eleanor passing through.

Letter to Reuben #3

Some things I remember that you don't:

1. Fighting fish. Looking in the mirror.

2. A playground tube, a couple making the moves. Making the moves.

3. Waffles and a truckstop. Salt shaker game.

4. I also know who won.

5. You punched Tony once when I wasn't looking I bet you don't remember that.

6. Old mining cave filled with old water. Swimming blind.

7. Later we lay in the sun for two hours or more we lay and lay.

8. Throwing rocks at the reservoir. I could never throw far.

9. There was a fence.

Eleanor

said her own name
outloud again after a long
hiatus and everyone cheered.

The ceiling fans that made
no noise themselves chopped claps
into more claps

creating the illusion that even more
people were clapping
clapping for Eleanor saying her name.

> *I will be a painter*
was the next thing
Eleanor said.

All this time she was standing in
          a plywood two-dimensional boat
          holding a three-dimensional parasol
          and apparently floating
on three rows of two-dimensional wooden waves
          painted sea-green
          set at varying heights to compensate for their two-dimensionality
          and rocked about by two men per wave offstage.

The waves multiplied in their movement
          took up more space than they ought
          and in that way they
          greatly resembled real waves

          or waves in a real painting
a painting of Eleanor
and water, warm,
warm like newly folded paper.

As my mother
did with children
Eleanor continued
  I will paint the paintings out of myself to make room for more paintings.

Thus began the self-portrait
    and the self-portrait of the self-portrait
      the autobiography
only if you squint
stop turning pages
brush over details.

Salt Flats

for Andy Smith

All this in the middle of winter
when the salt water
was colder than frozen and yet not frozen.

I saw you after I married Brian.
You were wearing a t-shirt with a drawing
of a man toasting with his beer—
Here's to all the virgins in the world:
Thanks for nothing.

The wedding picture was to be taken
on the salt white Utah flats
but there was lightning that day
and then someone said lightning is attracted
to the negative ions in the salt.
There was that story of skydivers
eight of them going down into the cold
salt in a tiny plane
the rainwater skimmed up on the surface.

No name #1

Thinking of you
Paul fills a childsized teacup
with pool water using
a childsized teaspoon
(this takes a while).
I sit still and a spider
begins a tiny web
on my arm hairs.
I sit in the sun (thinking of you)
and Paul fills a childsized creamer with pool water.
Brian cannons into the pool.
When I brush the spider off my arm
I accidentally rip it apart.

We all wear different nametags
(My name is Kathryn.
I am married to Brian.
His mom is Mildred.
She is an original Cragun.)
I am not myself today.
Many times removed.

The sky draws a line in the dirt
What a storm, blue and moving.
Blue like the summer only meaner,
only it looks me in the eye.

John teaches me how to trap wild animals as we run a particularly slow leg of the Snake River on a raft
Thirteen bald eagles. Four pair, two that are children.
That means three all by their lonesome.
John says one kind of bird catches a fish

by stabbing it clean through.
You ask, What are you afraid of?

Don't worry, I am OK
OK, OK, you caught me—
I'm still lifting my feet
when I drive over cow catches.
OK so long as I can run off.

Look me in the eye
A butterfly stuck to the windshield wipers
glares at me,
eyes on the back of its head.
I press mine into my pillow and try to sleep.

The cloud spills onto the mountain spills onto the road
Waterfalls and an avalanche of run-off
or a lake suddenly on top of the mountain.
All in a matter of seconds
and a flash flood catches a child off guard.

I read myself onto the landscape
The river splits around a full-on mountain,
the river swollen green with lonesomeness
having gnawed off its own leg
to get out of a trap.
The prospect of a reunion.
A letter from an old lover.
I drive far, far away.
I have a letter pressed up against my thigh.
The prospect of a letter.

Save yourself, that's what I say
You know I'm only going on about the Milky Way
because you reminded me of Eleanor.
You know every constellation
is E.
So many stars to start naming individual ones.
And everyone knew I didn't believe in marriage.
And kicking and screaming.
And Andy Smith is still mad.
And he couldn't save me.
Oh, the Milky Way. Lovely, lovely.
So many stars.

Andy Smith feeds his cat vegetarian cat food and is not pleased with the outcome
The cat has caught a butterfly,
rips out its gut.
Close your eyes.

Change your own damned name, I tell the landscape
I drive for Star Valley, for Salt River,
places someone clearly named to remind me
how far I am from my city.
I drive far, far away
so I can come back to you,
with your eyes so familiar
with the back of my head.

Two-headed (and with a knife)
The sky cuts itself down the belly,
a split personality,
one side sky blue, one side black and blue,
a Medieval painting of heaven and hell,
so that Jesus Christ descending
like there's no tomorrow
would not be out of place

and a cardboard cut-out of a cloud
could be an atom bomb.
Everything is splitting apart.
Close your eyes for a kiss.
(I know I will.)

Interview

Interviewer: I'm going to ask you a question. There is a right answer, and I'm very serious, and I want you to answer seriously. Seriously, but also honestly. Here is my question: What do you do if you find a dead cat?

Eleanor: Name it.

Interviewer: Wrong. What do you do if you find a dead cat?

Eleanor: Mouth to mouth, depending on the newness of its deceasedness, the likelihood of revivification, and whether or not it's an ugly cat.

Interviewer: Wrong again.

Eleanor: Was the cat on my property or my neighbor's?
Eleanor: Is it summer or another season?
Eleanor: Put it in the freezer to buy time.

Interviewer: No, no, no.

Eleanor: Light its cigarette.
Eleanor: Ask it to light my cigarette.
Eleanor: Brush its black, or grey, or tawny hair out of its eyes and shed a single tear.

Interviewer: Stop it. Lies, all lies.

Eleanor: Kill another cat so it has a friend.
Eleanor: Show it photographs of my children.
Eleanor: Actually, I have no children to show.

Interviewer: This is not at all what I had in mind.

Eleanor: Chalk a line around its silhouette for future reference.
Eleanor: Of course, I'm assuming the dead cat is on the ground. Really,

	it could be anywhere.
Eleanor:	Up a tree, or nailed to the side of a building.
Eleanor:	Utilize catnip in creative ways until it stops playing dead, that old trick.
Eleanor:	Wait for Jesus to come.
Interviewer:	You never say what I want you to say.
Eleanor:	Taxidermy.
Eleanor:	Halo its head, lend it my wings.
Eleanor:	Are you listening?
Eleanor:	Do you really want to know?
Eleanor:	You can learn a lot about a person by asking.

2

Timp,

 Timp,

 a mountain of woman
jumping off after her lover no waterfall to mark where

 night writ

 large across her broken back body

 small over my shoulders
 small of my back

Here it is my secret

1
I am bowling and I want my nickname
on the TV screen to be Circle K but it's written
Kathyizzle which by God which
I hate I hate it I don't even like the name Kathy plain.

A pregnant bowler called Pregnant Bowler is wearing her bra
on the outside of her dress. She chose the name.

I choose a red ball with a white target
not trying to convince myself
the pins are really going after the ball no.
What I'm trying to convince myself of is a secret.

2
My jacket has turned the color of cigarette smoke
we've been here so long.
I trust the cigarettes to make my jacket a pretty grey
and the man at the bar to call me what I call myself.

You say I trust too rarely I say my amaryllis
is growing a third stalk in a single season.

3
Eleanor, Andy Smith, the man at the bar.
Be literal-minded. Believe me.
Look at my fingernail and concentrate while I say
my fingernail that's what it is please go
ahead and touch if it helps.

4
I had forgotten I said goodbye to Andy Smith and to Portland outside a bowling
alley his car was going and his girlfriend was inside with a scarf around her waist
and wrist and one around her hair and I smashed my mouth into his neck our arms
pulling at each other smashing and trying to get closer because we knew although
we'd see each other again eventually we knew this

5

was goodbye Oh Andy Smith I said Oh
outloud not thinking
but now that I think about it
I could have been talking to any one
of a number of people named Andy Smith
in other cities on the face of the planet
and in that city even
where there are so many of them I can't keep track.

Drop in a bucket

Every pigeon in the world lands
on a rented house near here and
                    my mother has forgotten
                    that I am family.
A hole in my roof leaks
shingles to the wind and
                    I can't track down Andy Smith
                    his name is too common.
Grandma Elizabeth's rows of Queen Elizabeth Roses
revert to wild pink floribunda roots and
                    I lose Eleanor
                    to Christian fundamentalists in matching t-shirts.
Two burning bushes I failed to replant
blush red with awkwardness and
                    I need a scarf I buy a pink
                    cocktail dress with a broken zipper.
Grandpa tells a joke if you can't see Mt. Hood
through clouds it's going to rain and if you can it is and
                    I cry as the plane descends into Portland to know
                    there's too much beautiful beautiful.
Drops of rainwater pool in my closet
the floor wet with rooflessness and
                    I swoon at the name "Eleanor" at letters
                    in a name I try to stifle my swoon.
Red leaves play like roses but they always
fall goddammit nothing can stop them and
                    I have already begun
                    to rename my closest friends.
The smog-fog inversion layer is generous it gives
its whole body takes cities whole and
                    my mother's marriage changes her last name
                    I keep mine split family tree chop chop.
At mirror lake of 27 such I catch single
waterlilies among the hundreds and
                    I can't wash a scarf that smells like Andy's cigarettes it

is different from all the other scarves in the world.
Outside in the rain not two minutes when
wet leaves stick all in my hair little red moths and
                    I lose my letters to other Kathryns one
                    a scientist in Ohio I would fight her for them.
One tree holds seven leaves six five
the other some two hundred tight and
                    one leaf I pick from my hair
                    and hold and hold and hold and hang on my wall.

No name # 2

Eleanor's house
was full of new sounds you know
doves, coo, coo

When Reuben said what he said I knew he was history
I watched a plane fly all the way across the sky

Yes I think Yes Paul will call back
I think today is the day
Paul will call
I see a bank sign that spins
and says Today
I take this as a good sign

My mother
divinely translated from flesh and blood
a big billboard
that says Mother in big letters.
Big without body
and I did this to her

A new name, a new category, a baby bird
I will call it a Brian.
I will break a bottle of champagne
over its young head.
I will cut the really big red ribbon
with really big scissors.
Welcome, welcome, really, and
it is too late

I am sorry I hurt you, little poem
I wrote that for the baby bird

I am still 5 yrs married
and then some short days later oh my suddenly not

Whoosh it is a fast bank sign
Whoosh Today
I drive past again on purpose
so I can see it again
and take it as a sign
this time it says Holiday
and 1:45
Whoosh please be Today

Aye Aye
like a lady pirate
Eleanor looked
all sharp edges
old rusted copper in her eye
and one time I tried to hold her hand
follow my finger, dear,
look where I'm pointing
a
way

Geoff wants to go
to an island in Greece
like Grandma Elizabeth
if there is anywhere to find the thing I want

An island in Greece
blue and white and dark blue
it is easy to be in love

Edamame pretty word
we eat sushi out in the open for the first time you
are better at it than I
ceiling fans strange man at the sushi bar
you are better
Whoosh Whoosh

Bugs live in the dying mint
I have pulled the mint plants in from outside and made the bugs die
but I suspect others

Dead bugs come out to die
they are not dead when they come out, only after
that is the way I find them

A baby bird to cope
so be a baby bird
so I can take care of you
or take care from someone else if you can't take me or just
take care

And these people I don't know cut the grass
at my home that is not mine
my little apartment
is what is mine
no grass though
mint

The bloody sort of newborn chick
so little and hurt and slimed up

Inexplicably drawn to my blue sweater as I dress
I worry you are merely in love
with my coloring

Have done
what have I done, Oh
what have I done Oh what
have I done Oh what have
I done

I try to feed myself
Rachel agrees, yes, heat your food
to convince yourself you love you
I drink a breakfast drink
(it is not supposed to be heated)
but really I love me
more

Reuben invites me to visit his cabin
I think of him as Snow White
butterflies landing on his open palm
birds dressing him in aprons
Reuben doing his pushups on the front porch
to stay in shape he says
how can I visit
I do not think I can visit

Reuben assures me he is not on the prowl despite his very recent breakup
him and what army

Eleanor wished she had a flamethrower
she would use it for good
rather than evil

A re-present, a microwave, suddenly, mine once again
Brian has given it to me he agrees,
yes, heat your food to convince yourself,

it busts when I try to use it
also the fridge turns off
also my ice cream melts
my green pistachio

Reuben talks about the power
he has over me
wants to use it for good
rather than evil
him and what army yeah right

Paul calls today
out of nowhere
I let him leave
his message

Please believe me unbelievable
Please believe me
Oh what have
it's so easy to
love Oh have done

Transcript
Today I
discovered magical
properties of mint
green Look at me
when I'm talking to you

I can't help it I drive past
the bank again I turn to the same song
and try to get it to the same spot
Today say Today

I'm not making this up #2

a translation of Federico García Lorca's "Es Verdad"

You are a pirate. With a cage. What work. It costs me
to love you like you love. I say these things in neon lights.

For you. Love. Me, I fight the air first.
And my heart hurts.
And my hat as well.

Who are you anyway to play at unlocking this enormous metal door, like you have
 the money for it, the patience, like you have my heart, like you have its key, the
 original bag it came in, the receipt.
One hundred times. Over. Still Kathryn. This and every version. Dances the night
 away. Is the pretty
pretty princess of sad. Is the black angel. Sings along with Lou Reed.
Is annually white. No really, I mean it, once a year. Is making do. Is for the taking.

Good Lord, go away already.
Leave off. Have your cage. Your rat trap.

Poem with a real historic event at its end

I do not believe in confession but I must confess
I told two people I was done with writing Eleanor
and I am not.

Holy cow I am a bruiser.
I am a fighter I am a fuckup
I have a butter stain on my shirt.
Jesus Lord I can make my hand into a bird.

I can make the poems follow me
by playing my flute.
I would rather it was the other way around.

I can make my hand into a hand.
I confess I didn't really make it into the bird
that just happened and I saw it and wrote it down.
With the other hand.

Here's a handful, a whole handful just for you.
I pulled it all together with my bare fingers.

Here it is my historic event:
One of my hairs got stuck to your shoe.
It is nobody's fault. Nothing to cry about.
Nothing to write home.

I am happy in spite of everything nonetheless.
Measured in pistachio shells,
it has been a very good evening.

I must confess that the event involving the hair
was not terribly historic.
And that I knew this ahead of time and wrote it down anyway.

Here is a real historic event:
This guy died a guy I liked he was famous
his death was historic like Historic Fillmore
but bigger it was big and unprecedented.

I had never had to hang around my house
with him dead before.

Requiem in five parts
for Paul Cowles

1
A whole head grey
hair lips eyelids
cheekbones nearly visible
fine-threaded
tutu tulle from monster ballet
residue perhaps of
the Mt. St. Helens ash
you shoveled off the roof
heavy stuff that it was
to keep things from caving in
after a whole week in black and white
and grey and you—
the old meat of Greek mythology
the faulty phoenix
always leaving
never coming back
the hole in the mountaintop—
you weren't family anymore
after my parents split
but you nonetheless showed up
to my mother's place Christmastime
all grey and utterly, utterly

2
Passing through Pendleton city of wool
city at the foot of a brake-burning hill
my mom, my sister and I
learned the different parts to
"Down to the River to Pray"—
sang it in Columbia River fog
outside Portland proper
funeral-bound
appropriate somehow
that you are forever
a lotus eater

3

You would get up and go out
and not go to AA
where you said you could be reached
in the event of an emergency
but to a hollow rhododendron bush
in my grandmother's back yard
sometimes in the middle
of the night among
pink purple flowers
thriving on the soil's acidity
brown-bagged glass
I saw your footprint
on the desk under the window
it was almost too perfect, like your foot
wanted so badly to give you away

4

I closed the closet doors
where your clothes
still were for fear
that small parts
of you were still in them
for fear of spontaneous resurrection
of the confusion of you
finding me in your room
finding yourself stuck
on various articles of clothing—
for fear of the strange explanation I would have to give

5

My grandmother says she found you light
with a smile the mortician removed—
I wouldn't know I
hid outside the viewing said
I was looking after the kids
yours and my little sister
not likely you had gotten
any more grey
but I did not care to find out
assuming you had died heavy to have left such a mark

3

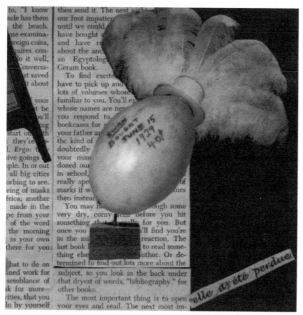

I drew a beauty
mark with eyeliner behind my left ear

arc to Arcturus
      speed on to Spica

                    Deneb   Vega
                                   Altair
              Dogstar
                    Sirius
                              Northstar
                    Bearstar
                                   Polaris

                              Ursa Major
                              Minor great
                              funeral procession in the sky

no, no sir

Out of Eleanor an egg

Eleanor dropping eggs from the roof in the evening
Made quite a mess
some split wide and spread
cracked to bits all over
and slicked the cement
clear egg white.

Eleanor with an egg
Hard to fit an egg
whole in the hollow
of her mouth
to swallow.

Out of an egg
Comes Eleanor
little yellow little beautiful bird.

An egg-dropping contest
Wrap your egg in a pillow
and drop it
it will hold together.

Hook your egg in a homemade holder
with rubber bands
it will not break.

Hold your egg hold it hard
hold it in your hands
and jump.

To believe in the solid
surface of white
one must have an egg white faith.

Telling Eleanor from Eleanor

in which the author describes how, though she has not seen them in the same room together, she knows they are not the same person.

a) Eleanor had joined a circus troupe and was touring. She was very small, much smaller than one would think. That was her act. It was big to think of Eleanor, small to see her. Contortionist, she had posters.

b) Meanwhile, completely elsewhere, Eleanor snapped her leg and later her head. To be fixed at the hospital where Brian's dad reads peoples' bones for breaks. Incidental which leg. Broke everything eventually.

c) So you see Eleanor and Eleanor are two distinct people in two different places at once not even close to the same.

d) Eleanor cut her hair short far sooner than Eleanor.

e) True, both are brunette. Lots of people are brunette.

f) Eleanor left her job at the bakery, and I discovered Eleanor working later at the same bakery.

g) Born again on a sofa, Eleanor was happy for the place to stay, and so God came easily. Eleanor begat immaculately. Born again.

h) She wrote me to say Lord knows when we'll meet again. Till we mee-ee-eet till we mee-eet. I had all the while been meeting secretly with Eleanor again and again and in fact Eleanor was with me while I chatted on the phone with her and that struck me as funny so I laughed out loud and Eleanor said oh good so you're happy so I'm happy.

i) There are some things I confuse. Sometimes I can't remember who.

j) And they do look alike.

k) Lost a leg in the war with her father lost her father lost her head Eleanor punched bag a finger hole the whole kitten Eleanor whom I loved and lost Lord knows if I've never seen them in the same room, it is only because they have never been in the same room.

Page from a dictionary

E•la•mite (e - le - mite) *n.* **1.** A native or inhabitant of Elam. **2.** The language of the ancient Elamites, of no known linguistic affiliation. [Elamite, from Middle Elamite *Eleam*, to speak, from Old Elamite *Elean*, to be spoken for, *Eleanic*, or God's tongue—divine intervention by way of the mouth, or God's divine pointer finger.]

é•lan (a - lan) *n.* **1.** Enthusiastic vigour and liveliness. **2.** Distinctive style or flair. **3.** A flare; a fire thrown from one's person. [French, from Old French *eslan*, thrown fire, from *eslancer*, to hurl: *es-*, out (from Latin *ex-*; see EX-) + *lancer*, to throw (from Late Latin *lanceanor*, to throw a lance, from Latin *elanceanor*, one who throws a flame, or flamethrower).]

e•lapsed time (i - lapst) *n. Abbr.* **ET.** The measured duration of an event: *Many years of time have elapsed (ET) since Eleanor left, since Eleanor sprang the big city.*

e•las•tic (i - las - tik) *adj.* **1.a.** Easily resuming original shape after being stretched or expanded; flexible: *She is not a hat but she stays on my head. She is not a blanket but she wraps around me.* **b.** Springy; rebounding. **2.** *Physics.* Returning to or capable of returning to an initial form or state after deformation: *She opens and opens and retains her shape after multiple washings.* **3.** Quick to recover, as from disappointment: *She had an elastic spirit but not, alas, an elastic effect.* —**elastic** *n.* **1.a.** A flexible, stretchable fabric made with interwoven strands of rubber or an imitative synthetic fiber. **b.** An object made of this fiber. **2.** A rubber band: *Eleanor stretched elastic between two fingers, said break, break, I mean it.* [New Latin *elasticus*, from Late Latin *eleastos*, beaten, ductile, variant of Greek *eleanos*, from *eleanon*, to beat out, to make, to break, as in break into essential parts, into pieces.] —**e•las•ti•cal•ly** *adv.*

e•las•ti•cized (i - las - ti - sizd) *adj.* Made with strands or inserts of elastic: *A skirt Eleanor made elasticized with a grandma waistline I love this unwearable.*

e•lect (i - lekt) *v.* **e•lect•ed, e•lect•ing, e•lects.** —*tr.* **1.** To select by a vote for office or for membership. **2.** To pick out; select. See Synonyms at **choose. 3.** To decide, especially by preference: *Eleanor-elect, elected official, I choose.* —**elect** *adj.* **1.** Chosen deliberately; singled out. **2.** Selected by divine will for salvation: *My pointer finger says only your name.* —**elect** *n.* **1.** One who is chosen or selected. **2.** *Theology.* One selected by divine will for salvation, as in Chinese finger trap. [Middle English *electen*, from Latin *eleactor*, *elean-*, to select: *e-*, *ex-*, *ex-* + *leanor*, to select, to choose for one's own, to take, to name, to rename for one's own, for one's own sake, to make; see **lean-** in Appendix, see **-nor**, see **either-or**.]

e•lec•tric (i - **lek** - trik) *adj.* **1.** Also **e•lec•tri•cal** (-tri-kel). *Abbr.* **elec.** Of, relating to, or operated by, electricity: *electric current*; *an electrical appliance*; *the electric air around her blurred body.* **2.a.** Emotionally exciting; thrilling. **b.** Exceptionally tense; highly charged with emotion: *My hair electric with her, without, balloons sticking to all the walls.* —**electric** *n.* An electrically powered machine or vehicle: *Eleanor's flamethrower is an electric.* [New Latin *electricus*, deriving from selection, attention, from Latin *eleactrum*, pay attention, from Greek *eleacnor*, *eleanor*, pay attention, pay attention to me.]

All this pink

Earlier in the day, I find what appears to be
the source of the entire world's electricity
in the Nevada desert outside Vegas—

poles and poles and electric wires
going out to all over the planet.
In the middle of it all, a woman in pink dictator suit
with gold chains on the shoulders proclaims
Let there be lights.
No one can say no.

That night as the sun sets pink
we walk down the new
Strip each of us with
a plastic Eiffel Tower full
of pink and frosty alcohol.

We hold our Eiffel Towers by the base
the man at Le Petit Bar tells us.

I hold mine like a baby on my hip.
You forget about holding the base and let yours
slip your hand slides fast up
the skinnier and skinnier part
and pops off the top
onto our shirts and the carpet.
All this pink comes out and out.

I see brides everywhere.
Hanging out in corners brides
out in the open with grooms brides
and others there's
a group of brides
dressed in pale sparkles and matching
shoes and eyes and veils and men

wearing matching brides matching
tuxedo T-shirts. Brides. Everything
smells like smashed up cigarettes and blown
bubble gum.

You say you have never wanted to be a bride
so much as now
and that this is a nice day
for a pink wedding. After all
it's always dusk in Paris
in Vegas.
I am a big pinkplastic-covered connector
wire and I want
all my fingers in all the lights
my drunken arms and legs and hairs
spilling out onto your shoulders my right arm
squeezing about your neck your left hand
grabbing at my shoulder blade
my forehead sweating out glitter
flavored pink alcohol
and both of us dizzying
at leggy fountains and
let there
and let there be and
let there be lights and all.

Poem in which The Dawn comes all over the city (which is not a pretty thing)
a translation of Federico García Lorca's "La Aurora"

New York's Dawn comes with
four columns of mud
and a storm of black words
that land like hats on all the people I've lost there.

New York's dawn is sorry
for all the people I've lost there,
offers to help me look, even.
Impossible work. Too little, too late. Angels and Andy Smith too good
   at hiding. Had a look around. No luck. No detective.

The dawn breaks and I take it in the mouth.
Just because. Morning is so impossible, and Eleanor is long gone.
One time I said I would pay to see Peter in the city.
Always leaving everyone or buying his poultry well I will pay

first thing in the morning, and I'm wet to the bone
with worry, which, rather like Eleanor, is neither here nor there,
and I have a number for Andy Smith but it is old and dirty,
my looking fruitless again halfhearted again and hidden under its hat

again morning comes. Finally. The light ruins me, and the city,
and science, and the roots connected to their leaves I am a wreck come back
   I am a wreck,
all the people in the streets, crowding, I am a wreck, insomniac,
a wreck I tell you, Angels and Andy Smith are in disguise for a spy flick,
   and I can't tell the difference, no detective, an absolute wreck, and Eleanor
   is a real killer.

All of this is connected, I tell you

A woman behind me is reading another woman's fortune on her hand and also on some cards

    in St. Stephen's Green, Dublin, a group of young musicians
    was taking turns at the violin, everyone clapping
    when they finished their rounds
    and I was clapping my hands and drinking tea in the sun
    loose leaves collecting in the bottom of my cup
    unreadable, nothing to see here

        my watch is broken, tells time all wrong, disconcerting
        like The Beatles singing I want to hold your hand in German

           already the grass is drying out asking to be burnt through
           really asking for it, for a fire, and I run
           all by myself asking for a fall into the fast river
           for a twisted ankle I run farther
           than anyone on the days
           when bicycles are not allowed in the canyon
           and don't run into a soul for an hour at least
           I run straight uphill

The palm/card reader has lines that say she undermines her own goals
but the woman whose hands she's reading does not have the lines
so that's something
                my own hands all foreign feeling all bit nails
                overlapping veins with creases
                on the underside like there's something growing there and
                I want them to be in my pockets

        my watch really is broken again, stopped running altogether
        can't bring myself to wear a new one
        if I hit it that sometimes does the trick
        or reset everything, the date day of the week 24-hour clock
        and just the regular time as well, so this takes a while you see

and I hit it again, still on my wrist, and I hit it again
and I hit it against my book but it's stuck
though marking the correct time now that it's reset
I can get the second hand to wiggle a bit if I shake it wiggle
wiggle and I look up and someone's
watching me

Chase me to a drop off. I will stop.
I will run at you.
I run into a trap just so I can snarl.
Hit me in the stomach Brenda said hit me in the arm.
How Houdini did it, how Houdini died.
Seeing stars.

Place clears, off goes the fortune teller, I get a good look and sure enough she is
wearing a scarf over her gypsy black and multiple necklaces, a look that inspires
confidence, I know she would have told me if my aura had a hole or flashing arrows

a new watch not in the stars
this one started stopping when my uncle died
when watches everywhere
lost seconds but no one was paying attention
his watch stopped too though that may have happened earlier
had lost track of time entirely by that point anyhow

How Houdini did it. Magic.

Uncle Paul's last months
day in day out
dress eat mac and cheese maybe
watch some TV undress bed
sometimes sleep on the couch
each day, disconcertingly
exactly the same
then came the day
with the squirrel
Paul said talked to him
good sign he'd run

out of time, talk
about a bad omen fuck

this watch is killing me hit it on my book again bite
my fingernails again all over again all this has all
happened already before

a man in a shady corner eating his bread and cheese by himself looks at me
puts his arm in the air like he has a question puts it down, what does that mean

tell time by the positioning
of the sun, tell home
by its proximity to the North Star
which is not so bright but well loved
because of its constancy, tell me
I am constant, or don't tell
constantly undermining
my own goals,
my dirty hands, read between
the lines, tell
the future by reading stars and
some bumps on my head are a war
are the first martyrdom and
something really bad in 200 years
tell me the color of my eyes
as I close them
don't tell me you forgot
didn't you say you were paying
attention, there, three more
seconds gone and you
didn't even notice and they're
green of course, green in part
tell me, tell me, you want to hold
my ha-a-and
tell you what
it's all happened before

Poem to Reuben #5

upon hearing that the reason he failed to return contact for a very long time had not so much to do with what the poet thought but more with the fact that he had got himself beat bloody by a gang of straight-edgers

1
I am not making this up.
I do not think Reuben is making this up
though one never knows.

2
That he emailed so soon after gives one pause.
That he bothered to tell me how his two teeth
are just now fixed, how some cuts took stitches.
Take care of yourself. Take care.

3
Because I don't know what he's getting out of this.
I only know what I'm getting out of this.

4
Because I want an economical exchange
and a fair market.

5
And who chugs beer in front of a gang of straight-edgers?
Some people are asking to be governed.
You could be the tallest jerk on the face of the planet.
This is only logic.

6
No that's not true what I said in 4
I want to be winning all the time.
Winning or holding reins,
bragging rights.

7

There is no room for bragging rights when Reuben
has got himself beat bloody, when Reuben has demonstrated
so persuasively he has not taken care.
You could be the tallest jerk on the face of the planet
and there would be no room. Logic dictates.

8

I do not have time to worry so.
Seven-foot-tall mythological figures
should be able to take care of themselves.

9

And then I don't know what I'm getting out of this.

No name #3

Middle of the night
My sides ache from a half bottle
of whiskey lo li lu
tender to the touch
hold me bottle my
your arm can fit my sides can wrap
and flip me upside down
my face against the bathroom tile
your cheek is cold
when I wake you from your black black head

Side of the freeway
I point at stars
so thick we can
lose the big dipper
stars not where I remember them
where my mother said
sad the rest of the drive blue

A handful of decimated raspberries
and I am writing it down again all of it
I can and you are peeling
oranges in the kitchen

Stars on the ground all the way up to my feet
My head aches from my neck
like someone's poking
but anyway I can see
all the city lights
from the top of a hill

Gale spelled like the wind
She asks me to describe
what it *feels* like to receive
a hyacinth from Geoff.
It smells good. I like the smell. I feel that
he put it in a pot
said he'd help me take care

There are more important things
Will it be the blue toothpick
in my special drink tonight
or the yellow
the most important decisions
I have to decide
today

Sweet potatoes / potatoes / onions / olive oil
all taste cooked sugary I lick your finger
I lick all my fingers
feel stuck no sticky

Not them I mean but me
The cold windows are fogged over, love,
watching you breathe
you make them think warm
or not worry anyhow

Stars like holes
where I looked too hard
gone, gone
but not so after all
when I look away

Happy in the library
I poke your leg under the table
to remind you
how happy

Laundry night
My wet clothes arranged on all the furniture
on which we are not presently sitting
room *feels* wet
I think how to tell Gale
I feel your curled hair
I feel blue but it doesn't mean sad
anymore no just blue.

Geoff kisses my shoulder
two times as I write
so I write
that down

Dear, I said, deer
he thought I said tear
as in I'm crying
that wasn't it
so I turned his head
and pointed
that thing   over there.

Eleanor, Eleanor

Eleanor, Eleanor, not your real name
Makes my poem important, I say
Eleanor, Eleanor, come back to my form

Eleanor, Eleanor, wrapped in my arm
Don't be Eleanor until I say
Eleanor, Eleanor, not your real name

Eleanor, Eleanor, don't you want a rhyme
To tuck in your hair, say
Eleanor, Eleanor, come into my form

Eleanor, Eleanor, lovely poem
Let me be the one to say
Eleanor, Eleanor, not your real name

Eleanor, Eleanor, be more of the same
Be in New York but be as I say
Eleanor, Eleanor, come into my form

Eleanor, Eleanor, so little time
To say the thing I want to say
Which is after all only your name
Eleanor, Eleanor, Eleanor

4

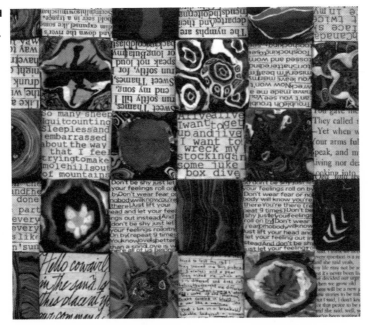

my missing writing book
collaged to pieces
by your pretty fingers
and glue

the Jesus
            inside cover
      the hands
            of my best friends
      cut from photographs
            we're all missing parts

Oh my

1
Love, you have caused my shoulders
to cling together across my back.

I will not stop writing just because
you have made me happy.
If I am happy, I will write that down.
And if I am not, well,
I still have the lovely sky
and Reuben is in his apron
and Andy Smith is playing bass guitar
and Eleanor, oh Eleanor,
Lord knows what happened.
Eleanor likes it that way.
And if Eleanor is happy,
so much the better for the world.

I lop off my left hand every day mid-wrist, love,
and I miss it, and your neck as well.
Take it, it is yours to shake.

2
My feet hurt, they hurt
from all this walking away
your eyes so familiar
with the back of my head.

Take me, I am yours to shake.
But I am not yours.

3
You are my Oregon, love,
you are my salt water my sweet sweet
my wrap of waves my punched
driftwood one-two.
I sit on the driftwood and think of you.

4

Oh baby, goes the song
Oh baby, and that's all I've got
worked out something about
Oh love, or was it
Oh my love.

5

All the trees lean in to touch my head
as a blessing because the world loves
me because I love you and the world
is so happy
the wasps
at the drinking fountain
chance their women's waists to brush their fat
abdomens on my cheek, aiming right into my eye
and dozens of tiny black flying bugs
with wings the size of bodies
have died drowned in the sweat on my chest
in your name because I love you
happy to go that way.

Poem containing a line from a song

Let's say I broke up my heart again. Let's say it's my own idiot fault. Let's say that although it was my heart, when it broke, I felt it in my stomach, like when I see a snake, and that it lasted for half an hour, and that I saw it coming.

Let's say I got stitches in my side again for the first time in months when I was running the next day, like leftover slivers stuck on my insides, let's say, it's the aftershake that wrecks the weakened sidewalk hours later. Not the earthquake.

I saw the Northern Lights for the first time from an airplane flying over an ocean, green and cold and cold and moving arbitrarily. Brian was asleep.

Aurora Borealis, the icy sky at night.

That's right.
That's it exactly.

Baker's sugar snow

Wet on my neck
sticks to my scarf.
You take yours off
as the car heater kicks in.

City with its head
in the clouds but clear streets
some ten feet high. City weighed
down by thick white.

No one is keeping you here.
Let me drive you to some other
place. I have nothing to say.
Talk about the weather.

It is hot outside and inside as well

1
Robert Creeley is dead
and reading a poem to me
from a recording he made
in his kitchen.

2
And a man in the canyon has been thrown
from his motorcycle
heavier looking because horizontal
and I think he is dead.
They are putting a blanket over him and it is 110 degrees.

3
And a really big fire means no electricity
two poles down
it is hot outside it is hot
with three-hundred-thousand kids at the pool
somewhere between Vegas and Mesquite
a motorhome burned to where
it was a foot tall and Paul
had to turn off his air conditioning
because of the traffic and how hot the car got

4
Last night I sat out gawking
there are a lot of stars
to be so sad
something I loved has a hand around its wrist

5
And how I want air conditioning
like I want my mouth on the palm of your hand I want that
salt on my mouth and to see the fire from the freeway
like I want a nice long run

and to meet Robert Creeley for the first time
I want eggs and green olives from the store
the fire to go out
my hand around the wrist of the something I loved
like I want a dead guy to walk away smiling
to tell a really good joke
like I want to walk away
to be universally loved and admired
and for the universe to go on and on and not look back over its shoulder
and to sing for a large crowd tonight
to sing to know where I am
like I want to return to my salt city
and not look back over my shoulder
and I want to go on a nice long run the same as the last one only no snakes and
    maybe get a little farther up the canyon this time
like I want to be universally loved and admired
or at least to have a nice day tomorrow or Tuesday would work too

6
A flipped car and I swear I saw
a hang-glider fly right into the mountainside.
I write that I want to go home with my finger in all caps on my thigh
which means I want to go backward in time
which makes me smile.

Wake

for Paul Cowles

1
the sun behind you
makes you thin
nearly
see-through
your head all light

2
think, think me
newly 20 in
the freezing waves
of the Oregon coast
with your boy (my cousin)
waist high and shivering
goosebumped hair on end
and walking still farther out
sun setting
over the water
seagulls like winks
and night getting dressed

and then me
in the same spot
with my father
sitting on driftwood
not cold so long
as we don't
change positions
the sun almost blue
honey yellow wine
still buzzing in our heads
laughing and stopping
to be very,
very serious

and then not so again
and changing positions
when the sand
gets cold

still later me
at the double window
above the freeway with
your mother
the whole Columbia River valley
open to us the bridge
to Vancouver the sailboats the bend
watching airplanes
lift from PDX
lift
and lift
and move away

the beach
has shifted slightly
when Brian and I return
honeymooning
(Brian whom you never met)
we open a bottle
of champagne
cheers to you
on a picnic table
by the sand line
too scared
we'll break
some glass antique
in our pretty room
we never find the top
after it bursts
we are clearly drunk
and trying not to act so

all this now

3
the air is thin
like past the tree line
on Mt. Hood
or in arms
or up in arms
my hair
previously wet
dries in salty tangles
and curls
changing places
with the air around it
the sun
eats away
warmly at my sides
I turn
stare directly
at it

El El El Eleanor

1
Eleanor, Eleanor, can't cut you out
you are still here
now and now and still now.

2
Eleanor is a stutter I keep spitting her
Ella el Elea Elenea N nn nor either or
everything I say is.

3
Here I go again Eleanor.
And one more time for now Eleanor.
Eleanor I can't help myself Eleanor.

4
Sometimes a silent Eleanor like h
sometimes very small but always
still very Eleanor.

5
And then I got a letter from
Eleanor whom I love very much
or from Eleanor five years ago that is

6
Eleanor is in New York City and she's happy and she believes she's happy and she
believes in God and she wants everyone to believe in God everyone including me
and I don't think I will write back.

7
Not much anyway. A little
I can't help myself.

5

I let off a helium balloon

from my elementary school with a letter inside and a check mark yes and
my address there were hundreds of balloons uniform orange and brown go
grizzlies

and the sky moved
and the ground

An epistolary conversation with Eleanor
altered somewhat but largely intact

I:
that I did think she was crazy and I hoped she didn't mind.

She:
It is well.
It is enough to know even as I am known, to love, to be, and be alive, to be awake in the dream, to fly, to see.

I:
that it was good to know she (or it) was well.
that it was good to know her words were having orgasms without her.
that it was clear to me from what she wrote she was still crazy.

She:
I may be moving to meet some things new, people new, god new in the days that are shared in the breath of sea feel try do.

I:
that she would have written, before: See.

She:
I am the rain and you are the wind and last night there was a reunion. I was there, in the dark outside—dark, because the moon was covered by thick clouds—in my underwear and remembering you (though the underwear is unrelated, I thought it was a nice part). And you were there in spirit, but in body I suppose you were at home in bed.

She:
There is no stopping now and here is now and here is where we begin.

She:
I'll see you when it is perfect to see you, and perfect for you to see me. God knows when that is, always seeing you in the place where there is no distance between. Bye. Love,

And then her name.

Goodbye poem
for Peter who has moved and who left me his office

What looks like a forgotten pomegranate
bit through flesh melting and exposed
in my new desk drawer
is really a painted tree decoration
on a gold string.
You have left it for me.
A coffee maker also.

You planted hydrangeas in your yard
and they are dying
too big even for this big place
so that the green fenced ground
chokes them out.
And I don't think anyone has been watering them.

On my porch a snail
has outlined a footprint shape
over and over
a snail is all foot I have heard
so this makes sense
the circle the starting again
the leaving behind
the liquid trail to mark
where you've been.

I have glued my shoes back together.
There is an umbrella stand
in my car trunk.
I want you to know these things
to know why I am so happy.

You are beautiful in New York City.
You are beautiful walking into buildings
reading and crowding the streets

and buying your water and chicken.
I want you to know I think you
are so beautiful
I would pay to see it.

6. On her dress, Eleanor has a body

a translation of Blaise Cendrars's "6. Sur la Robe Elle A un Corps" from Dix-Neuf Poèmes Élastiques

Eleanor's body has bumps to read like my head
And put to the same glorious use
I've tried to incarnate her spirit
But writing her body up is such a dirty job
Stupid with phrenology
My eyes are the only measurement of her sensuality and when they
    catch one thing, another thing blurs

So I'm always moving back, stopping, moving closer she wears her
    insides out
Her stars give a tour of the sky
Her colors disrobe
<<On her dress, Eleanor has a body>>
Her arms, legs, fingers, moon-shaped nails watery eyes de-verse
    themselves like she's turning her back, her cold shoulder
Even her belly is a spinning disk that's budging away
When I call her breasts a color they turn rainbow
Belly
Disk
Sun
I write her name into a right angle and the colors drop suddenly
    from her thighs
ELEANOR ELEANA ELLE ELLIE all names turn into

She's the one with the hands that reach out
She's driving the train has all the holidays all the eyes all the
    fanfares all those who live in one bar or another
And on her hip
The signature of no poet

No name #4

Eleanor in my gold chair
with the Chinese pillow
says to me so you have your own
apartment now
ran into Brian with another
put two and two
I love my own apartment
Eleanor's never been
works at a bread bakery
and I keep missing her

A pothole out my window
causes cars to splash
water at my screen
snow has fallen
I can tell by the sound

Made an angel in the snow
cement parking lot love
to leave a shadow behind love
to make you smile
hair wet and pulled back
with snow legs wet
and pulled back
and forth and snow
angel always wearing a dress
and with a very small head
always looking up
everything looking

Went to buy a sandwich from Eleanor
shop closed no such luck

no shot to see the flour on her face
to kiss both cheeks
and how long her hair
Eleanor in my gold chair
Eleanor soon enough

Geoff can barely leave me
magnet that I am
to do his laundry take a shower
take my time
take it, I have extra

On my back and moving
up toward the sky
snow standing still I think this
is to fly
and it
takes
no effort

Eleanor in my gold chair
has a lollipop
cherry flavor
that's bad, very bad,
looks at her picture
and I love Geoff

Geoff can barely keep his hands
wants to make me change
my underclothes
makes a good faith effort
strong showing
there are things I can see
well enough
alone

Photographs of her not her
all over so she has
been here not here
or is always
what a resemblance
Brenda says even with
all the little
punches of holes
and I can still tell El
Eleanor oleander
white with soft
and winged

A small ice-skating rink
outside my window
slip or take care
but not from me
who am careless

Geoff kisses me
oh baby makes me want
to change
all the time in the world

I can see the clouds move because the mountains stay still

A helicopter hurtles itself through the sky armless
leading with its mouth and beautiful eyes
and nothing to break a fall nothing.

Mountains make the pools of saltwater
look like holes in the ground
through which you can see mountains.

A man on the horizon is an optical illusion
with legs twice the size
of the rest of his body
or he's on stilts but really
he's just walking on water.

The water is thin no Jesus this one
from far away
throwing things into the salt
one thing so hard so high it never comes down.

Postcards

Dear Eleanor,
I noticed today the milk turned
two days overdue it turns out
reminded me of you
I thought I'd write though
I don't know
where you've gone.
Yours truly,

Dear Eleanor,
Sat in the sun
today reading soft gay porn
I hope you get this
before your mother
I'm sending it to her address
can't think of any other place.
See you around,

Dear Eleanor,
Lost that picture of you
with mosaic circles
pressed in the plaster
wall behind your head
a moving halo that passes the edge
of the photograph
and keeps moving out
your feet floating
a medieval painting
a Madonna.
Anyway it was out of focus.
Sincerely,

Dear Eleanor,
Till my skin
is green and rotted
till I need oranges like I need chewable Vitamin C
like I need my heart
till my compost head makes me sing
and my legs fall off green and my fingers
till I'm all over eye-colored and lovely
till then.
Love from,

Dear Eleanor,
I know you were here earlier
today some signs you left
on my porch chair
a hair a page from the Bible
the core of an apple
and you threw dandelions into my yard
next time stay longer at least just until I come back please don't go.
xoxo,

About the Author

Kathryn Cowles is finishing her PhD in Creative Writing at the University of Utah with an emphasis in Poetry. She is co-editor of poetry for *Quarterly West* and co-chair of The Working Dog reading series, and has published poems and essays in *Colorado Review, Pleiades, Barrow Street, Octopus*, and elsewhere. She lives in Salt Lake City with poet Geoffrey Babbitt and their dog Adeline.